1930	Robert Ashley b. (d.2014); Tōru Takemitsu b. (d.1996); Veljo Tormis b. (d.2017)	
1931	Carl Nielsen d. (b.1865); Sylvano Buss b.; Sofia Gubaidulina b.; Mauricio Kag b. (d.2008)	
1932	Alexander Goehr b.; Rodion Shchedrin b.; John Williams b.; Per Nørgård b.; Pauline Oliveros b. (d.2016)	
1933	Henryk Górecki b. (d.2010); Krzysztof Penderecki b.; Morton Subotnick b.	…lla, Dallapiccola *Partita*
1934	Edward Elgar d. (b.1857); Gustav Holst d. (b.1874); Harrison Birtwistle b.; Peter Maxwell Davies b. (d.2016); Alfred Schnittke b. (d.1998); Christian Wolff b.	Hindemith *Mathis der Maler*; Shostakovich *Lady Macbeth of Mtsensk*
1935	Alban Berg d. (b.1885); Giya Kancheli b.; Terry Riley b.; Helmut Lachenmann b.; Arvo Pärt b.; Kurt Schwertsik b.; La Monte Young b.	Gershwin *Porgy and Bess*; Messiaen *L'ascension*
1936	Richard Rodney Bennett b. (d.2012); Cornelius Cardew b. (d.1981); Steve Reich b.; Wang Xilin b.	Berg Violin Concerto; Prokofiev *Peter and the Wolf*
1937	Maurice Ravel d. (b.1875); Ivor Gurney d. (b.1890); George Gershwin d. (b.1898); Philip Glass b.; David del Tredici b.; Valentin Silvestrov b.	Webern Variations for Piano; Berg *Lulu*
1938	John Corigliano b.; Frederic Rzewski b.; Joan Tower b.; Charles Wuorinen b.	Barber *Adagio for Strings*; Stravinsky 'Dumbarton Oaks'
1939	Louis Andriessen b.; Jonathan Harvey b. (d.2012); Barbara Kolb b.; Ellen Taaffe Zwilich b.	Bartók Violin Concerto No. 2; Cage *Imaginary Landscape No. 1*
1940	Silvestre Revueltas d. (b.1899); Julius Eastman b. (d.1990); Frank Zappa b. (d.1993)	Britten *Les Illuminations*; Rodrigo *Concierto de Aranjuez*; Tippett Concerto for Double String Orchestra
1941	Frank Bridge d. (b.1879); Haflidi Hallgrímsson b.	Messiaen *Quartet for the End of Time*; Rachmaninov *Symphonic Dances*
1942	Meredith Monk b.	Shostakovich 'Leningrad' Symphony No. 7; Strauss *Capriccio*
1943	Sergei Rachmaninov d. (b.1873); Brian Ferneyhough b.; HK Gruber b.; Robin Holloway b.; Morten Lauridsen b.; David Matthews b.; Roger Smalley b. (d.2015); Tania León b.	Krása *Brundibár*; Ullmann *Der Kaiser von Atlantis*
1944	Cécile Chaminade d. (b.1857); Ethel Smyth d. (b.1858); Amy Beach d. (b.1867); Peter Eötvös b.; York Höller b.; Karl Jenkins b.; Michael Nyman b.; John Tavener b. (d.2013)	Bartók Concerto for Orchestra; Copland *Appalachian Spring*; Ginastera *Cinco canciones populares argentinas*
1945	Béla Bartók d. (b.1881); Anton Webern d. (b.1883); John Rutter b.	Britten *Peter Grimes*
1946	Manuel de Falla d. (b.1876); Michael Finnissy b.; Gérard Grisey b. (d.1998); Colin Matthews b.; Pēteris Vasks b.	Strauss *Metamorphosen*; Boulez *Douze notations pour piano*
1947	John Adams b.; Laurie Anderson b.; Tristan Murail b.; Salvatore Sciarrino b.; Howard Skempton b.	Duruflé Requiem; Crumb *Three Early Songs*; Weill Street Scene
1948	Claude Vivier b. (d.1983)	Strauss *Four Last Songs*; Cage *Sonatas and Interludes*
1949	Richard Strauss d. (b.1864); Kalevi Aho b.; Eleanor Alberga b.; Poul Ruders b.; Kevin Volans b.	Messiaen *Turangalîla-Symphonie*

Continued at back

Series 117

This is a Ladybird Expert book, one of a series of titles for an adult readership. Written by some of the leading lights and outstanding communicators in their fields and published by one of the most trusted and well-loved names in books, the Ladybird Expert series provides clear, accessible and authoritative introductions, informed by expert opinion, to key subjects drawn from science, history and culture.

The Publisher would like to thank the following for the illustrative references for this book:
Page 9: Alan Berg and Anton Webern © gettyimages; page 21: Dmitri Shostakovich and Sergei Prokofiev © gettyimages; page 25: Sergei Rachmaninov © gettyimages; page 49: © Kapuo Kikkas; page 51: Karlheinz Stockhausen courtesy of Kathinka Pasveer via Wikimedia Commons and Kaija Saariaho © gettyimages / Raphael Gallarde

Every effort has been made to ensure images are correctly attributed, however if any omission or error has been made please notify the Publisher for correction in future editions.

MICHAEL JOSEPH

UK | USA | Canada | Ireland | Australia
India | New Zealand | South Africa

Michael Joseph is part of the Penguin Random House group of companies
whose addresses can be found at global.penguinrandomhouse.com

 Penguin
Random House
UK

First published 2018

001

Text copyright © Fiona Maddocks, 2018

All images copyright © Ladybird Books Ltd, 2018

The moral right of the author has been asserted

Printed in Italy by L.E.G.O. S.p.A.

A CIP catalogue record for this book is available from the British Library

ISBN: 978–0–718–18786–6

www.greenpenguin.co.uk

Twentieth-Century Classical Music

Fiona Maddocks

with illustrations by
Jeff Cummins

Ladybird Books Ltd, London

On the brink: the last romantics

By 1900 symphonic music had become enormous, lush, ready to fall like overripe fruit. Orchestras were vast. Composers such as Austrian Gustav Mahler and German Richard Strauss added offstage bands, thunder machines and cow bells, squeezing ever more players on stage.

Their ambitions were epic. Mahler wanted his music to embrace all mankind and nature. His 'Symphony of a Thousand' (No. 8, 1910), for an immense orchestra, three choirs and eight soloists, is a celebration of the human spirit. Strauss's mighty *Alpine Symphony* (1915) depicts a mountain climb complete with dawn, sunset, mist, storm and glacier.

The Russian Sergei Rachmaninov, a melancholic tunesmith of the highest order, painted in rich orchestral colours. So too did his countryman Alexander Scriabin. In his *Poem of Ecstasy* (1908) – which sounds exactly like its name – he addressed the whole cosmos, no less.

In France, Claude Debussy revolutionized – not too strong a word – music with fluid structures and sensuous, gauzy textures. In Britain, the choral tradition held sway: Edward Elgar's *Dream of Gerontius* was premiered in Birmingham in 1900, teetering between old styles and new. Samuel Coleridge-Taylor's *Hiawatha's Wedding Feast* (1898) was an immediate hit. In America, Scott Joplin, the 'king of ragtime', triggered new jazz syncopations. Western classical music was on the brink.

LISTEN: Mahler, Symphony No. 5 (1901–2)

New directions at the opera

The operatic century – a story in itself – dawned in 1900 with Giacomo Puccini's *Tosca*, likened by one critic to a 'chainsaw movie': the opera's heroine murders her sexual predator. Soon after came *Madama Butterfly* (1904), in which a young Japanese girl is exploited by an American lieutenant.

No rebel but with a keen grasp of the zeitgeist, Puccini wrote taut, realistic dramas with impassioned music and raw emotional content. These works remain favourites today.

Richard Strauss, at the forefront of German opera and a contemporary of Freud, injected the new psychology into ancient stories. Married to a soprano, he knew how to create strong female characters. Women rule, but not always nicely.

In his *Salome* (1905), the nymphet dancer of the Bible kisses the lips of the prophet, whose severed head lies bleeding on a dish. The music is lurid, voluptuous and gritty. His *Elektra* (1909) is built obsessively round the same few notes. It's a long but thrilling cry of expressionist agony.

In his influential *Pelléas et Mélisande* (1902), Debussy weaves a mysterious tragedy from a gossamer skein of music. Leoš Janáček's *Jenůfa* (1904), featuring infanticide, shows a dark side of Czech village life.

It wasn't all misery. Franz Lehár's operetta *The Merry Widow* (1905) portrays a decadent Old Europe, merrily drinking champagne and waltzing all the way to bankruptcy.

LISTEN: Richard Strauss, *Salome* (1905)

Breaking free: Vienna – rethinking tonality

Innovator, theorist, guiding light of the avant-garde and, in his own words, 'musical bogeyman', Arnold Schoenberg wanted a radical new grammar of music. With his important pupils Alban Berg and Anton Webern, this Austrian trio is known as the Second Viennese School (the first being Haydn, Mozart and Beethoven).

Together they pioneered 'atonality', which abandoned old assumptions about the way notes relate to each other. This meant an end to major and minor harmonies, the standard formulas of expression in Western music for three centuries.

With all twelve notes of the scale in play – all the black and white keys of an octave on the piano – this technique was called 'twelve-tone'. Schoenberg's Five Pieces for Orchestra (1909) and *Pierrot Lunaire* (1912) were of this new breed. The instrumental line-up changed: instead of massed strings and armies of woodwind or brass, single instruments had equal voices.

In its starkness and rigour, this music chimed with the unadorned Wiener Moderne style of the time. Architect Adolf Loos, Schoenberg's friend, designed the 'building with no eyebrows'.

By the 1920s Schoenberg had developed a yet more formal approach called serialism – a series of chosen notes informing a whole work, almost like a computer code. For some it became a liberating force. For all it was a catalyst for change.

LISTEN: Schoenberg, Five Pieces for Orchestra (1909)

Riots and rhythm: Paris – *The Rite of Spring*

In May 1913 a musical event shook Paris. Igor Stravinsky described his new ballet as the 'sound of nature renewing itself'. Others used ruder words: 'barbaric', 'primitive', 'jagged', even 'obscene'.

Written on the eve of the First World War for Diaghilev's Ballets Russes, *The Rite of Spring* caused uproar at its premiere. Most of that initial fuss was about Nijinsky's erotically convulsive choreography. At times the mockery was so loud the music became inaudible – hard to imagine for so noisy a work.

The Rite is steeped in Russian folk song. It makes rhythm, rather than pitch, paramount. Try counting 1, **2**, 3, **4**, 5, 6, 7, 8 (emphasizing the bold numbers). Listen to the stomping string music soon after the piece starts and you'll recognize that pattern, as rhythm is heaped on thudding rhythm.

Generations of composers name *Le sacre du printemps* (its original French title) as their biggest influence. Many heard it first thanks to Walt Disney, who thought it 'perfect for prehistoric animals' and used it in the film *Fantasia* (1940). The British composer George Benjamin called this 'atavistic primitivism' seminal.

Stravinsky, still only thirty, would cut his way through the century like an angle grinder through granite, as did his artistic equal, friend and some-time collaborator Picasso. Stravinsky remains the lodestar of twentieth-century music.

LISTEN: Stravinsky, *The Rite of Spring* (1913)

1914–18 The Great War: composers at the front

No single style is associated with the First World War. Its splintering of cultural life and old concert habits changed the way music was performed, cross-fertilizing with jazz, dance and music hall.

The rat-a-tat opening to Gustav Holst's *The Planets*, written in 1914 before armies clashed, foresaw the approach of war. He followed this with a powerful choral elegy to the fallen, *Ode to Death* (1919), setting words by the American poet Walt Whitman.

The poet-composer Ivor Gurney expressed his homesickness for Gloucestershire in songs such as 'In Flanders'. The melodic gifts of George Butterworth, untouched by Schoenberg's experiments, were silenced by his death on the Somme. Every country had its Butterworth.

The French composer Maurice Ravel, too old for active service, worked as a driver on the Western Front. His wistful, delicate piano piece *Le tombeau de Couperin* (1914–17) is a memorial to friends who died in battle. Stravinksy's *The Soldier's Tale* (1918) encompasses all the weary agony of the marching life.

Alban Berg's freely atonal opera *Wozzeck* (1914–22) is about an abused, low-ranking soldier. Berg wrote: 'There is a good bit of myself in this character, since I pass these war years equally dependent on detested people, tied, ailing, unfree, resigned and even humiliated.'

LISTEN: Berg, *Wozzeck* (1914–22)

March of the women: sisters in art

Where were the women? In the parlour playing the piano? From standard accounts you would think so. Female composers had difficulty getting their music performed. When the English composer Rebecca Clarke won a prize anonymously, the judges assumed she was a man.

Ethel Smyth wrote the suffragettes' campaign song 'The March of the Women' (1911). She spent time in Holloway Prison, where – usually the only fact known about her – she conducted her march with a toothbrush through the bars. Brahms met her. He was guarded: 'So this is the young lady who writes sonatas and doesn't know counterpoint!'

The American symphonist Amy Beach had to negotiate with her own husband, who restricted her public appearances (as a pianist) but allowed her to compose, which at least could be done in private.

Sisters Lili and Nadia Boulanger made a double impact. Lili died young, leaving a few radiant compositions. Nadia became a revered and feared teacher. Her pupils included Aaron Copland, Elliott Carter, Astor Piazzolla, Leonard Bernstein, Pierre Boulez and Philip Glass, all part of this tale, and also – less expectedly – a master of smooth melody, American songwriter Burt 'Magic Moments' Bacharach.

LISTEN: Lili Boulanger, *Faust et Hélène* (1913)

Jazz and the sounds of the city

Cars, radios, phonograph records. The Charleston, the Black Bottom, the Flea Hop. The French called the Roaring Twenties the *années folles* (crazy years). Others preferred the Jazz Age or the Machine Age.

Debussy and Stravinsky had already borrowed from jazz. Erik Satie's ballet *Parade* (1917) used 'noise-instruments' such as typewriters and lorry wheels. Composers were, as ever, on the hunt for new sounds. Anything you could hit or bang would do.

The Paris-born Edgard Varèse wrote *Amériques* (1918–21, revised 1927) in tribute to his new homeland. Sirens screech. Foghorns blare. That later experimentalist John Cage said Varèse 'fathered forth noise into twentieth-century music'.

European classical music also caught the cross-rhythms of swing, bebop and blues. Ravel wrote a ragtime duet for teapot and teacup. Bohuslav Martinů, a Czech in Paris, toyed with tangos and foxtrots. Arthur Honegger celebrated locomotion in his orchestral work *Pacific 231* (1923). George Gershwin, on a train to Boston with its 'steely rhythms, its rattle-ty bang', dreamt up his *Rhapsody in Blue* (1924).

The ultimate all-arts triumph was Nijinsky's ballet *Le train bleu* (1924): music by Milhaud, text by Cocteau, costumes by Coco Chanel, front curtain by Picasso. *Quel cocktail!*

LISTEN: Gershwin, *Rhapsody in Blue* (1924)

Nationalist tendencies and folk revival

Many composers rediscovered the value of folk music. This oral tradition – songs of seasons and ritual, of work in fields or factories – was in danger of being lost.

Béla Bartók first noted down a Hungarian folk song as early as 1904. He believed music should serve the brotherhood of nations and took equal interest in Slovak, Romanian, Arab and other traditions. Not all composers were quite so democratic.

New sound recording devices, as well as sharp-eared fieldwork by the likes of Zoltán Kodály and Ralph Vaughan Williams, helped preserve this dying art. Often these collector-composers arranged more sophisticated versions, as with Vaughan Williams's *Fantasia on Greensleeves* (1934).

Manuel de Falla reflected Hispanic traditions in his lovely *Seven Spanish Folk Songs* (1914). In France, Joseph Canteloube gathered songs under the title *Chants d'Auvergne* (1923–30). His orchestrations may be somewhat cloying, but they made his name. Across the Atlantic, Ruth Crawford Seeger preserved and arranged American folk songs. Stravinsky plundered Russian folklore all his life.

The English folk revival, with its whiffs of Merrie England, met with mixed reactions. Cecil Sharp founded the English Folk Dance and Song Society, still an invaluable resource for traditional songs and dance tunes, though the enthusiasm for Morris dancing has never been universally shared.

LISTEN: Kodály, *Dances of Galánta* (1933)

The shadow of Stalin

In 1917 Lenin's Bolsheviks swept to power in Russia.
Stalin succeeded him and took a harsher view of individual
artistic freedom. By 1932 socialist realism had become the
mantra for Soviet culture. This meant populist, accessible,
optimistic works promoting the socialist state.

For the two chief composers of this era, Sergei Prokofiev
and Dmitri Shostakovich, artistic life was a constant and
terrible game of cat and mouse.

Shostakovich was a favourite of the Soviet regime until
1936, when his opera *Lady Macbeth of Mtsensk* was
condemned as ideologically dangerous and banned. He
rescued himself with his Fifth Symphony (1937), a work
of greater accessibility and simplicity, as he put it, though
not without darkness. His life continued to be dogged by a
repression experienced by other Eastern bloc composers.

Prokofiev was subjected to similar treatment. After
pursuing an international career in Europe and America,
he returned, homesick, to Russia. He had success with
Peter and the Wolf (1936) and, after wrangles, with his
rhythmically exhilarating ballet *Romeo and Juliet* (1938).
Yet he remained under surveillance. He died on the same
day as Stalin, in 1953.

Another voice from the period is that of Shostakovich's
pupil (he proposed marriage to her more than once) Galina
Ustvolskaya. At once brutalist and religious, her music –
which includes five symphonies – was almost entirely
silenced until the USSR collapsed.

LISTEN: Shostakovich, Symphony No. 5 (1937)

degenerate — Coined by Nazis

Entartete Musik: a journey into darkness

When the Nazis came to power in Germany, all progressive art came under attack, even retrospectively. Anything abstract or avant-garde was condemned as degenerate and un-German. Jewish artists were censored, including composers of the past, such as Mendelssohn and Mahler. Communists were denounced for their beliefs. Many musicians, performers and composers alike, had already fled the country.

An exhibition called 'Entartete Kunst' ('Degenerate Art') in Munich in 1937 was followed – in Düsseldorf the year after – by one dedicated to music. The idea was to distinguish between the politically and ethnically 'pure' and 'degenerate'.

Ernst Krenek's dissonant, jazzy satire *Jonny spielt auf* (*Jonny Strikes Up*, 1927), about a black band leader, enjoyed success worldwide in the freedom of the Weimar years but was castigated by the new regime. A reworking of the sheet music's cover, replacing a carnation with a star of David and turning Jonny into a monkey, was used as the 1938 exhibition catalogue cover. It became an icon of degenerate imagery.

A group of Czech-Jewish composers, including Pavel Haas, Hans Krása and Viktor Ullmann, wrote music in Terezin (Theresienstadt) concentration camp. All three died in Auschwitz in 1944. A survivor described Ullmann as shy and self-effacing, qualities evident in his thoughtful music, which, like that of his confreres, is now being valued and played.

LISTEN: Ullman, Piano Sonata No. 7 (1944)

Exiles: New York and Hollywood

By the late 1930s many European musicians had emigrated to New York and Hollywood, Stravinsky, Kurt Weill and Schoenberg among them, the last famously captured on film playing tennis in Beverly Hills with Gershwin.

Rachmaninov and Bartók, neighbours on Manhattan's Upper West Side, wrote their final masterpieces there: Rachmaninov his *Symphonic Dances* in 1940, old Russia mixed with blue notes, Bartók his showpiece Concerto for Orchestra in 1943.

Melody surfaced in the Golden Age of Hollywood soundtracks. Erich Korngold led the way. Schoenberg, who wrote a score for an imaginary film, and Stravinsky too, were wooed by the studios but neither had the celluloid knack.

Others understood the demands of the movies and prospered: Franz Waxman (*The Bride of Frankenstein*, 1935; *Sunset Boulevard*, 1950), Max Steiner (*King Kong*, 1933; *Casablanca*, 1942; *Gone with the Wind*, 1939), Miklós Rósza (*Ben-Hur*, 1959), Bernard Herrmann (*Psycho*, 1960).

Some of the most experimental soundtracks, using early electronics for chase scenes or animal squawks, were for animated cartoons; Bugs Bunny and Looney Tunes, by Carl Stalling, also helped introduce classics to new generations.

Hanns Eisler and Bertolt Brecht's *Hollywood Elegies* (1942) summed up the gold-rush mood with this couplet: 'Gold in their mountains, oil on their coast; dreaming in celluloid profits them most.'

LISTEN: Korngold, Violin Concerto (1945)

Neoclassicism: old bottles, new wine

Weighed down by the constant mood of experiment and change, some composers found refuge in music of earlier times. The chance to restore certainty, balance and clarity into their work invigorated them.

This loosely labelled movement was active from 1920 to 1950. Our ears may recognize the light-textured patterns but the harmonies are new.

Prokofiev's 'Classical' Symphony No. 1 (1915) mirrors music by Haydn and Mozart but with 'wrong' notes. When Stravinsky made his *Pulcinella* ballet (1920), borrowing from an eighteenth-century composer, he said, 'the remarkable thing [. . .] is not how much but how little has been added or changed'.

Classical antiquity became a cultural fashion, as in Ravel's ballet *Daphnis et Chloé* (1912) or Satie's melodrama *Socrate* (commissioned in 1916 by the Princesse de Polignac, racy heiress to the Singer sewing-machine fortune).

Spurred on by Satie, and the artist-writer Jean Cocteau, a group formed in Paris known as Les Six. These young composers – including one woman, Germaine Tailleferre – each with their own distinctive musical style, were against most things: Wagner (music too overblown and epic), Debussy (too lush), serialism (too complicated). Wit, elegance and jazz were their thing. Fun while it lasted.

LISTEN: Villa-Lobos, *Bachianas Brasileiras No. 5* (1938–45)

Britten and the British – the land with music

The mid twentieth century saw an outburst of British music which continues into the twenty-first. There had been no absolutely top-rank composers between Purcell in the seventeenth century and Elgar two hundred years later.

Then several came along: William Walton, versatile, capable of stirring if conservative music (*Belshazzar's Feast*, 1931; symphonies, ceremonial and film music), Michael Tippett, a dreamer who folded blues into tough modernism (*A Child of Our Time*, 1944; *The Midsummer Marriage*, 1955) and, the most widely celebrated, Benjamin Britten.

His *Peter Grimes* (1945), taken from a poem by the Suffolk poet George Crabbe, ushered in a new epoch for English opera and established Britten's reputation. His partner, at a time when homosexuality was illegal, was the tenor Peter Pears. He sang the title role of the social misfit fisherman, one of many Britten wrote for him. In 1948 Britten and Pears spearheaded the Aldeburgh Festival in Suffolk, now an important international event.

By the 1960s a younger generation of radical British composers was forging ahead. Peter Maxwell Davies and Harrison Birtwistle were students together in Manchester. They experimented with fresh genres, inspired by Stravinsky and the latest guru-on-the-block, Pierre Boulez, as well as music from the neglected Middle Ages and Renaissance: all free from rules or expectations.

LISTEN: Britten, 'Sea Interludes', *Peter Grimes* (1945)

Greetings from **Aldeburgh**

Darmstadt: adventures in cults and schisms

The German city of Darmstadt was devastated by Allied bombing in the Second World War. In a quest for renewal, an International Festival for Contemporary Music was founded in 1946 – in the early years covertly funded by America's CIA as part of a cultural propaganda war.

Soon it became a high-profile meeting place for composers in the heart of post-war Europe, flourishing in the 1950s and 1960s. Those who came helped to shape the eclectic sounds of the twentieth century. To outsiders, Darmstadt looked like an avant-garde cult ruled by serialist orthodoxy. Internally there was hot debate and often schism.

Stravinsky, now in his sixties and living in California, felt his music had no place in this brave new world: these composers were, he noted, 'a generation which biologically [seems] to be hostile to me. What to do?' What he did was enter a serialist phase of his own with works such as *Agon* (1953–7).

Electronic music burgeoned, via tape recorders, electronic instruments and computers. Karlheinz Stockhausen emerged as Darmstadt's sorcerer-mentor.

'[Music] has taken upon itself all the darkness and guilt of the world,' wrote the critical theorist and composer Theodor Adorno. When he failed to understand a particularly thorny piano piece (by another Darmstadt composer), Stockhausen retorted: 'Professor, you are looking for a chicken in an abstract painting.'

LISTEN: Nono, *Variazione canoniche* (1950)

Tunes please, we're American

What is American music? European traditions long dominated in the concert hall, but gradually vernacular styles of jazz, swing or folk crept in. The waspish critic-composer Virgil Thomson summed up: 'All you have to do is be an American and write any kind of music you wish.'

Aaron Copland, Samuel Barber and Leonard Bernstein were proud to be US originals. Copland, who studied in Paris but soon rejected the avant-garde, captured the American landscape with hoedowns and hillbillies in *Billy the Kid* (1938) and *Appalachian Spring* (1944).

Barber, from an old American family who might have preferred him to be a footballer, favoured romantic, sonorous music. His *Adagio for Strings* is one of the most famous pieces of American concert music, used in film and TV scores from *Platoon* (1986) to *The Simpsons* and *South Park*.

The New Yorker Bernstein made Manhattan street life famous with his sizzling *Romeo and Juliet* musical *West Side Story* (1957). Its string of hits include 'I Feel Pretty', 'Maria' and 'Somewhere', with words by an unknown whizz-kid, Stephen Sondheim. A brilliant conductor and educator, Bernstein left a noisy, charismatic stamp on the century.

After decades of neglect, a school of mid-twentieth-century African-American composers, such as symphonists William Grant Still and Florence Price, is back in the repertoire.

LISTEN: Bernstein, *West Side Story* (1957)

US mavericks: chance encounters

Chance and indeterminacy were key tools for John Cage. The American experimentalist had been a pupil of Schoenberg and Nadia Boulanger. Artistically he was their polar opposite. He believed any sound – motor, wind, heartbeat, landslide – could constitute music.

He wasn't the first. New Englander Charles Ives, little known in his lifetime, freely explored cluster harmonies and music without bar lines. Californian Harry Partch constructed instruments from bamboo, light bulbs and large Pyrex cloud chambers. He also used a microtonal scale of forty-three unequal tones (imagine notes 'in the cracks between the piano keys'). Conlon Nancarrow wrote zany canons for player-piano – virtuosity beyond the virtuoso.

Rejecting European complexity, Cage followed Zen principles and the I Ching. His most famous work was the silent riddle, *4'33"* (1952). Its point? To make people listen. 'Why do they start talking when there is something to hear?' he asked. He found allies among the painters Jasper Johns and Robert Rauschenberg and dancer Merce Cunningham.

Newcomers like Morton Feldman and Pauline Oliveros also explored silence and chance. British experimentalist Cornelius Cardew joined the party with his Scratch Orchestra and *The Great Learning*. Graphic scores extended the possibilities of music notation. Art and music met head on.

LISTEN: Cage, *Sonatas and Interludes* (1946–8)

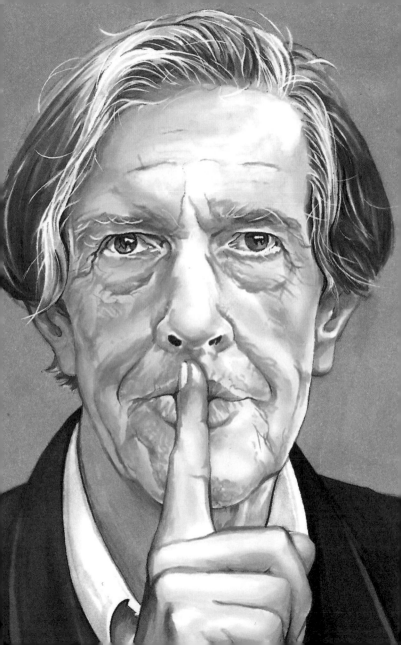

Sacré et profane: Messiaen and Boulez

Two contrasting French composers, with a fond regard for one another, cast a double spell over the mid century.

Olivier Messiaen was a visionary, a devout Roman Catholic and, for six decades, organist at La Sainte-Trinité in Paris. Inspired by Hindu rhythms and Balinese gamelan, he startled the world with his erotic *Turangalîla-Symphonie* (1946–8). This extravaganza features the eerie, whooping ondes Martenot, one of the earliest electronic instruments (later a favourite for film scores, and used by Jonny Greenwood and Radiohead). Messiaen wanted to create thousands of chords 'matching the sounds of birdsong'. Preoccupied with musical evocations of eternal time – as in his most popular piece, *Quartet for the End of Time* (1941) – he mixed serialism with tonality, symmetry with repetition.

Pierre Boulez, Messiaen's pupil, was an atheist, a perpetual enfant terrible, determined to take music out of the museum. As a young radical, Boulez pushed twelve-tone music to its limits. Busy conducting and teaching, he adopted an 'open work' strategy, keeping many scores permanently unfinished. He applied his fierce intellectual discipline to all he did, once describing himself as the dog barking outside the tent.

His *Le marteau sans maître* (1955), for contralto and six instruments including guitar and vibraphone, intricately woven, defying the linear, is a modernist classic.

LISTEN: Boulez, *Le marteau sans maître* (1955)

Hard stuff: electronics and concrete music

With so many technological advances, pitch and rhythm could be manipulated, speeded up, slowed down, played backwards, given spatial dimensions via speakers. Music no longer relied on someone playing an instrument in real time from a single source.

Varèse's *Poème électronique*, written for Le Corbusier's stomach-shaped pavilion at the 1958 Brussels World Fair, was a turning point. Sounds include taps, grating, 'airplane rumble', sirens and animal noises. In Paris, Pierre Schaeffer introduced the term *musique concrète*. The aim was 'to collect concrete sounds, wherever they came from'.

The Greek composer Iannis Xenakis, once Le Corbusier's architecture assistant, shocked audiences with his orchestral *Metastaseis* (1955). He made music out of stochastic mathematical processes. Think of slow shifts of mass in motion, gas clouds, probability theory, the flocking of birds. Or just listen to the amazing, evolving textures.

Everyone was at it, no one more spectacularly than Stockhausen in his Cologne studio, another Mecca of sonic novelty. The two-hour, four-channel *Hymnen* (1966–7) established his wider fame. Pop embraced his discoveries. The Beach Boys made *Pet Sounds* in 1966. The following year the Beatles included him on the cover of *Sgt. Pepper* – immortality indeed.

LISTEN: Varèse, *Poème électronique* (1958)

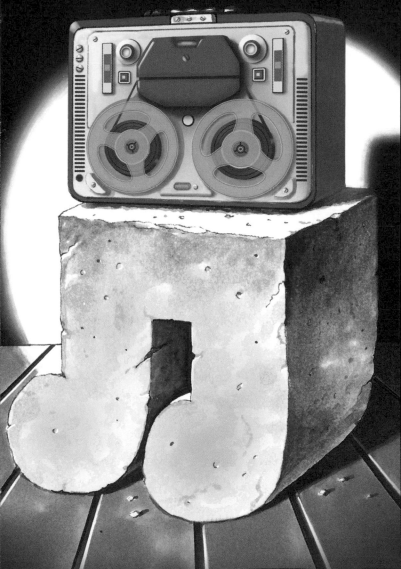

Anything but opera: music theatre

As the century progressed, traditional opera was dismissed as expensive and stagnant. The Hungarian György Ligeti called it irrelevant. Boulez said, 'The Paris Opera is full of dust and crap,' and wanted all opera houses to be blown up (though later he capitulated and conducted operas himself, notably by Wagner).

Yet the urge to match music with drama survived. As writers, like William S. Burroughs with his cut-up books, challenged narrative and French New Wave cinema rejected Hollywood, so composers made subversive stage works. 'Make it new!' as poet-musician Ezra Pound proclaimed.

Luigi Nono was the first avant-gardist to produce an opera, *Intolleranza* (1961). Neo-fascists, judging it to be anti-opera, protested at its Venice premiere. Hans Werner Henze yielded to his romantic tendencies in fourteen operas, from small (*Elegy for Young Lovers*) to large (*Bassarids*).

The anarchic Argentine Mauricio Kagel developed the idea of musicians moving and acting as they play. In 'Eine Brise' (1996), a 'musically enriched outdoor sports event', 111 cyclists ride along ringing bells, hooting horns and singing. Don't try it down your street.

The Irish composer Gerald Barry continues the absurdists' challenge. His *The Importance of Being Earnest* (2010) requires forty plates to be smashed. In perfect rhythm, of course.

LISTEN: Ligeti, *Le Grand Macabre* (1974–7, rev. 1996)

More cluster than group: European freethinkers

In a world less bound by artistic orthodoxy, strong individual voices emerged. The emphasis now was on timbre (or sound quality) and tone clusters (adjacent notes sounded together, as when you press your forearm on a piano keyboard).

The Polish composer Krysztof Penderecki used tone clusters in *Threnody for the Victims of Hiroshima* (1960). His fellow countrymen Witold Lutosławski and Andrzej Panufnik invented their own singular harmonic styles, in music of luminosity and subtlety. Another sensual loner-individualist, the Frenchman Henri Dutilleux shared similar attributes.

In contrast the Italian Luciano Berio created a labyrinthine, postmodernist style, bristling with allusion. His kaleidoscopic *Sinfonia* (1968–9) incorporates snippets of Bach, Mahler, Boulez, texts from Martin Luther King, James Joyce and Samuel Beckett, and student protest slogans from May '68.

Another progressive figure was György Ligeti. He came under the spell of Stockhausen but then favoured micro polyphony: static layers of sound and cluster-based harmony to create texture (*Atmosphères*, 1961). Stanley Kubrick borrowed Ligeti's *Requiem* (1963–5) for his film *2001: A Space Odyssey* (1968). Ligeti called his music 'democratically elitist – a music open to all, to which access requires enterprise'. A wise motto.

LISTEN: Lutosławski, *Mi-parti* (1976)

Ghosts in machines: IRCAM and spectralism

In 1971, Stravinsky died. Boulez told the *New York Times* obituarist: 'The death of Stravinsky means the final disappearance of a musical generation which gave music its basic shock at the beginning of this century and which brought about the real departure from Romanticism.'

Stravinsky had lived into the age of electronic music but never tried it himself: 'My dear, I know what electronic *sound* is [. . .] But electronic *music* . . . I don't know what that is.'

Fortunately Pierre Boulez did. Internationally regarded as a cultural wizard, he masterminded IRCAM (L'Institut de Recherche et Coordination Acoustique/Musique). This electro-acoustic sound lab, wedged next to the new Centre Georges Pompidou in Paris, opened in 1977. Many composers used its sophisticated software, Frank Zappa, Harrison Birtwistle and Jonathan Harvey among them.

An influential group working at IRCAM, including Gérard Grisey and Tristan Murail, were known as spectralists. Their focus was sound, rather than notes or harmonies. A younger generation – Pascal Dusapin, Julian Anderson, Rebecca Saunders – has followed their lead. The French-Romanian composer Horațiu Rădulescu referred to 'sound plasma', comparing it to the blue image of Earth as seen from outer space. Put like that, the concept may be easier to grasp.

LISTEN: Grisey, *Les espaces acoustiques* (1974–85)

Play it again and again: minimalism

Minimalism was a revolt. The American Philip Glass scorned the avant-garde as 'a wasteland, dominated by these maniacs, these creeps, who were trying to make everyone write this crazy, creepy music'. His target was a Boulez-led concert series in Paris. Feelings ran high.

A pulsating style became the craze, on the West Coast and via the New York-based artists' group Fluxus (Cage, Yoko Ono and the like). Out with serialism, in with chords, arpeggios, long forms. Californian Terry Riley's *In C* (1964), fifty-three note patterns repeated against a fast pulse by any number of players, was a landmark. La Monte Young, born in a log cabin in Idaho, experimented with drones.

Glass and Steve Reich, each with huge cult followings, had their own ensembles. Glass gained stardom with Music in 12 Parts (1971–4), *Einstein on the Beach* (1976) and *The Qatsi Trilogy*. Reich, using tape loops, phasing and West African drumming techniques, bewitched audiences with *Drumming* (1970–71), *Clapping Music* (1972) and *Different Trains* (1988).

The Velvet Underground, Brian Eno and Lou Reed fell under the spell. Julius Eastman and Meredith Monk pushed at minimalist boundaries. Louis Andriessen initiated a Dutch-led systems movement. John Adams developed a more subtle recipe and gave opera new force as political theatre with *Nixon in China* (1987) and *The Death of Klinghoffer* (1991). No composer liked being called minimalist. The word stuck.

LISTEN: Reich, *Music for 18 Musicians* (1978)

Less is more: holy minimalism

As the noisiest century in history neared its end, technology had made music available to all, as well as inescapable. Quietude became urgent. With the fall of the Berlin Wall in 1989, composers from the former Eastern bloc – Estonian Arvo Pärt, Russian Sofia Gubaidulina, Latvian Peteris Vasks – were free to let their repressed spirituality flourish.

Nicknamed 'holy minimalists', they favoured purity of sound and slow, open-note music. Symmetry and silence were key elements. Pärt went into retreat, inventing his bell-inspired 'tintinnabuli' technique: 'The complex and many-faceted only confuses me, and I must search for unity.' His *Fratres* (1977) and *Magnificat* (1990) bear this out.

Henryk Górecki had success with his *Symphony of Sorrowful Songs* (1977), which came – belatedly and to the Polish composer's bafflement – to symbolize the united Europe. In the UK, John Tavener, whose *The Whale* (1966) had grabbed the Beatles' attention, embraced the Russian Orthodox religion. His style of mysticism caught the public mood, especially after his 'Song for Athene' (1993) was performed at Princess Diana's funeral. BBC News noted: 'Materialistic, with a taste for cars and the best French restaurants, Tavener is also deeply spiritual.'

Ambient music, chanting monks, the therapeutic meanderings of Ludovico Einaudi, topped the charts. Max Richter was starting out. These new genres, blurring 'art' music and pop, would explode in the next century.

LISTEN: Pärt, *Magnificat* (1989)

Out of the auditorium, into the sky

A desire for the big experience prompted extreme musical adventure as the twentieth century closed. In Stockhausen's *Helicopter String Quartet* (1995), four pilots flew four musicians into the skies above Amsterdam. Sawing strings imitated roaring engines. It was an immediate hit, if somewhat tricky to stage.

Shape-changing ensembles – London Sinfonietta, Bang on a Can – met composers' unpredictable needs. Buzzwords divided and ruled: new complexity, new simplicity, new romanticism, new eclecticism. Mark-Anthony Turnage reinvigorated opera with *Greek* (1988). Thomas Adès invoked techno-dance and the ecstasy-fuelled club scene in *Asyla* (1997). The South Korean Unsuk Chin, one of an emerging throng of women composers, forged East–West styles. Finland's Kaija Saariaho and Denmark's Hans Abrahamsen and Per Nørgård signalled an eclectic Nordic wave.

On 31 December 1999 the Berlin Philharmonic, whose global fame owed so much to twentieth-century recording technology, played Schoenberg and Stravinsky: twin peaks of the century. At London's Millennium Dome, Tavener's ethereal *A New Beginning* was premiered, if anyone could hear it amid the partying. Next morning, the Vienna Philharmonic (still all-male) played traditional New Year's Day waltzes as if untouched by the revolutions of the century. Everything changes. Everything stays the same. The river of music runs on.

LISTEN: Adès, *Asyla* (1997)

Year	Births and deaths	Significant compositions/premieres
1950	Kurt Weill d. (b.1900); James Dillon b.	Boulez Piano Sonata No. 2; Schoenberg Psalm 130 'De profundis'
1951	Arnold Schoenberg d. (b.1874)	Goeyvaerts Sonata for Two Pianos; Menotti *Amahl and the Night Visitors*; Stravinsky *The Rake's Progress*
1952	Hans Abrahamsen b.; Gerald Barry b.; Simon Bainbridge b.; Heiner Goebbels b.; Oliver Knussen b.; Wolfgang Rihm b.; Kaija Saariaho b.	Cage *4'33"*
1953	Arnold Bax d. (b.1883); Sergei Prokofiev d. (b.1891); Florence Price d. (b.1887); Georg Friedrich Haas b.; Zhou Long b.; Chen Yi b.; Giorgio Battistelli b.; Robert Saxton b.	Bernstein *Wonderful Town*; Britten *Gloriana*; Stockhausen *Kontra-Punkte*
1954	Charles Ives d. (b.1874); Betty Olivero b.; Anders Hillborg b.; Judith Weir b.	Lutosławski Concerto for Orchestra
1955	Arthur Honegger d. (b.1892); Pascal Dusapin b.; Ludovico Einaudi b.; Bright Sheng b.	Boulez *Le marteau sans maître*; Xenakis *Metastaseis*; Martinů *Gilgameš*
1956	Gerald Finzi d. (b.1901); Sally Beamish b.	Cage *Radio Music for 1–8 radios*; Vaughan Williams Symphony No. 8
1957	Jean Sibelius d. (b.1867); Marie-Joseph Canteloube d. (b.1879); Elena Kats-Chernin b.; Tan Dun b.	Bernstein *West Side Story*; Poulenc *Dialogues des Carmélites*; Stravinsky *Agon*; Schoenberg *Moses und Aron*
1958	Ralph Vaughan Williams d. (b.1872); Magnus Lindberg b.; Esa-Pekka Salonen b.; Bent Sørensen b.; Julia Wolfe b.	Stockhausen *Gruppen*; Berio *Sequenza 1*
1959	Bohuslav Martinů d. (b.1890); Heitor Villa-Lobos d. (b.1887); James MacMillan b.	Elizabeth Maconchy *The Sofa*; Poulenc *La voix humaine*
1960	George Benjamin b.; Detlev Glanert b.; Osvaldo Golijov b.; Aaron J Kernis b.; Mark-Anthony Turnage b.; Jocelyn Pook b.; Rachel Portman b.	Barraqué *Au delà du hasard*; Boulez *Pli selon pli*; Zimmermann *Die Soldaten*
1961	Percy Grainger d. (b.1882); Unsuk Chin b.; Brett Dean b.; Jake Heggie b.; David Sawer b.	Babbitt *Composition for Synthesizer*; Ligeti *Atmosphères*; Nono *Intolleranza*; Poulenc *Gloria*
1962	Hans Eisler d. (b.1898); Jacques Ibert d. (b.1890)	Kagel *Heterophonie*; Tippett *King Priam*
1963	Francis Poulenc d. (b.1899); Paul Hindemith d. (b.1895); Thomas Larcher b.	Henze Symphony No. 4, No. 5; Stravinsky *Abraham and Isaac*
1964	Alma Mahler d. (b.1879)	Berio *Folk Songs*; Riley *In C*
1965	Edgar Varèse d. (b.1883); Henry Cowell d. (b.1897); Thierry Pécou b.	Gerhard Concerto for Orchestra; Ligeti *Requiem*; Reich *It's Gonna Rain*
1966	Kui Dong b.	Barber *Antony and Cleopatra*; Stockhausen *Telemusik*; Stravinsky *Requiem Canticles*
1967	Zoltán Kodály d. (b.1882); Julian Anderson b.; Olli Mustonen b.; Rebecca Saunders b.	Akutagawa *Orpheus of Hiroshima*; Cardew *Treatise*; Schuller *Triplum*
1968	Olga Neuwirth b.; Roxanna Panufnik b.	Berio *Sinfonia*; Birtwistle *Punch and Judy*
1969	Victoria Borisova-Ollas b.; Jóhann Jóhannsson b. (d.2018)	Cage *HPSCHD*; Maxwell Davies *Eight Songs for a Mad King*